GRAPHIC LIBRARY™

P9-DYE-890

INVENTIONS AND DISCOVERY

ELI WHITNEY AND THE COTTON GIN

by Jessica Gunderson

illustrated by Gerry Acerno, Rodney Ramos,
and Charles Barnett III

Consultant:
Regan Huff
Special Projects Consultant
Eli Whitney Museum

Capstone
press®

Mankato, Minnesota

Graphic Library is published by Capstone Press,
1710 Roe Crest Drive, North Mankato, Minnesota 56003.
www.capstonepub.com

Printed in the United States of America in Stevens Point, Wisconsin.

072015
009125R

Books published by Capstone Press are manufactured with paper containing at least 10 percent post-consumer waste.

Library of Congress Cataloging-in-Publication Data
Gunderson, Jessica.
Eli Whitney and the cotton gin / by Jessica Gunderson; illustrated by Gerry Acerno, Rodney Ramos, and Charles Barnett III.
p. cm.—(Graphic library. Inventions and discovery)
Summary: "In graphic novel format, tells the story of how Eli Whitney invented the cotton gin, and the effects it had on the South"—Provided by publisher.
Includes bibliographical references and index.
ISBN–13: 978-0-7368-6843-3 (hardcover)
ISBN–10: 0-7368-6843-7 (hardcover)
ISBN–13: 978-0-7368-7895-1 (softcover pbk.)
ISBN–10: 0-7368-7895-5 (softcover pbk.)
1. Whitney, Eli, 1765–1825—Juvenile literature. 2. Inventors—United States—Biography—Juvenile literature. 3. Cotton gins and ginning—Juvenile literature. I. Acerno, Gerry, ill. II. Ramos, Rodney, ill. III. Barnett, Charles, III ill. IV. Title. V. Series.
TS1570.W4G86 2007
677'.2121092—dc22 2006026399

Designer
Jason Knudson

Colorist
Cynthia Martin

Editor
Aaron Sautter

Editor's note: Direct quotations from primary sources are indicated by a yellow background.

Direct quotations appear on the following pages:
Page 9 from *Memoir of Eli Whitney, Esq.* by Denison Olmsted (New York: Arno Press, 1972).
Pages 19 and 22 from *The World of Eli Whitney* by Jeanette Mirsky and Allan Nevins (New York: Macmillan, 1952).
Page 23 from *Eli Whitney and the Birth of American Technology* by Constance McLaughlin Green (Boston: Little, Brown, 1956).

TABLE OF CONTENTS

CHAPTER 1
The Seeds of an Idea 4

CHAPTER 2
The Cotton Gin Is Born 10

CHAPTER 3
A Stolen Idea 18

CHAPTER 4
The Cost of a Dream 24

More about Eli Whitney and
the Cotton Gin 28
Glossary 30
Internet Sites 30
Read More 31
Bibliography 31
Index 32

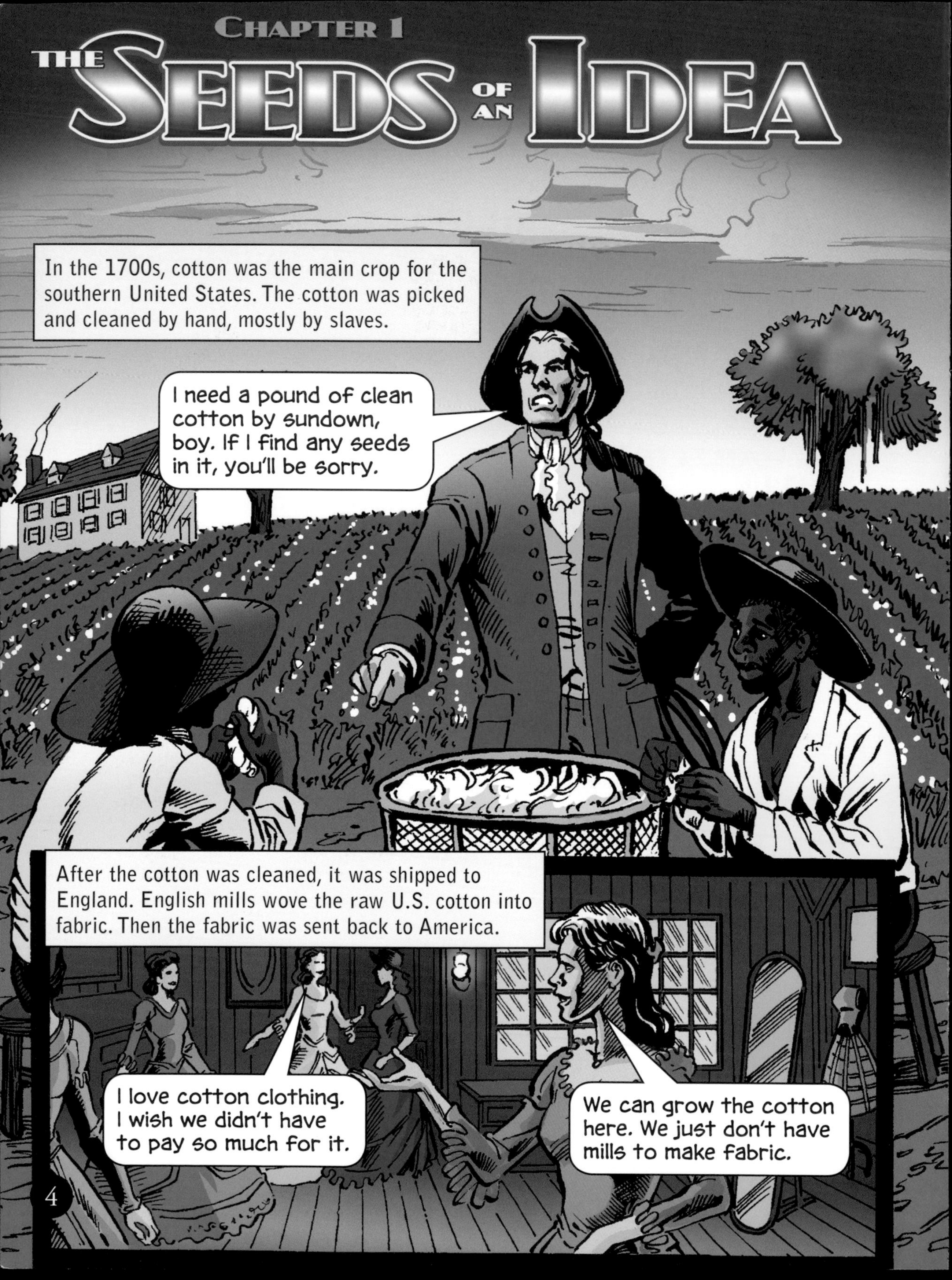
CHAPTER 1
THE SEEDS OF AN IDEA
In the 1700s, cotton was the main crop for the southern United States. The cotton was picked and cleaned by hand, mostly by slaves.
I need a pound of clean cotton by sundown, boy. If I find any seeds in it, you'll be sorry.
After the cotton was cleaned, it was shipped to England. English mills wove the raw U.S. cotton into fabric. Then the fabric was sent back to America.
I love cotton clothing. I wish we didn't have to pay so much for it.
We can grow the cotton here. We just don't have mills to make fabric.

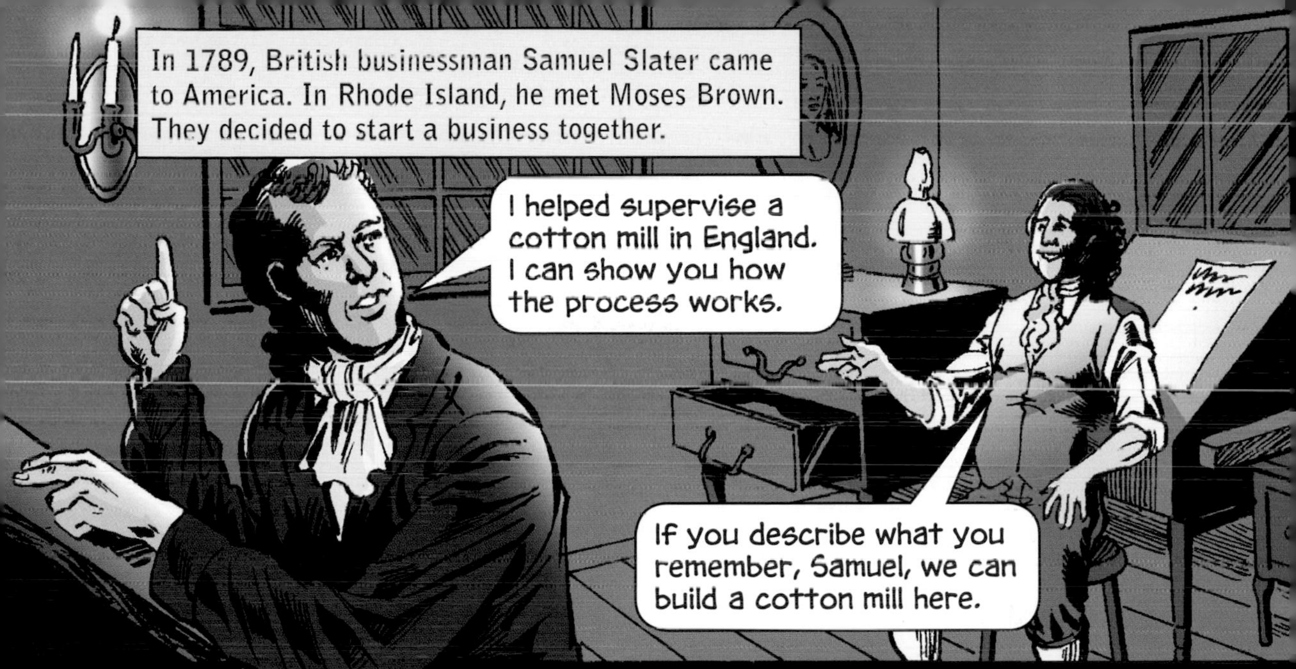
In 1789, British businessman Samuel Slater came to America. In Rhode Island, he met Moses Brown. They decided to start a business together.
I helped supervise a cotton mill in England. I can show you how the process works.
If you describe what you remember, Samuel, we can build a cotton mill here.

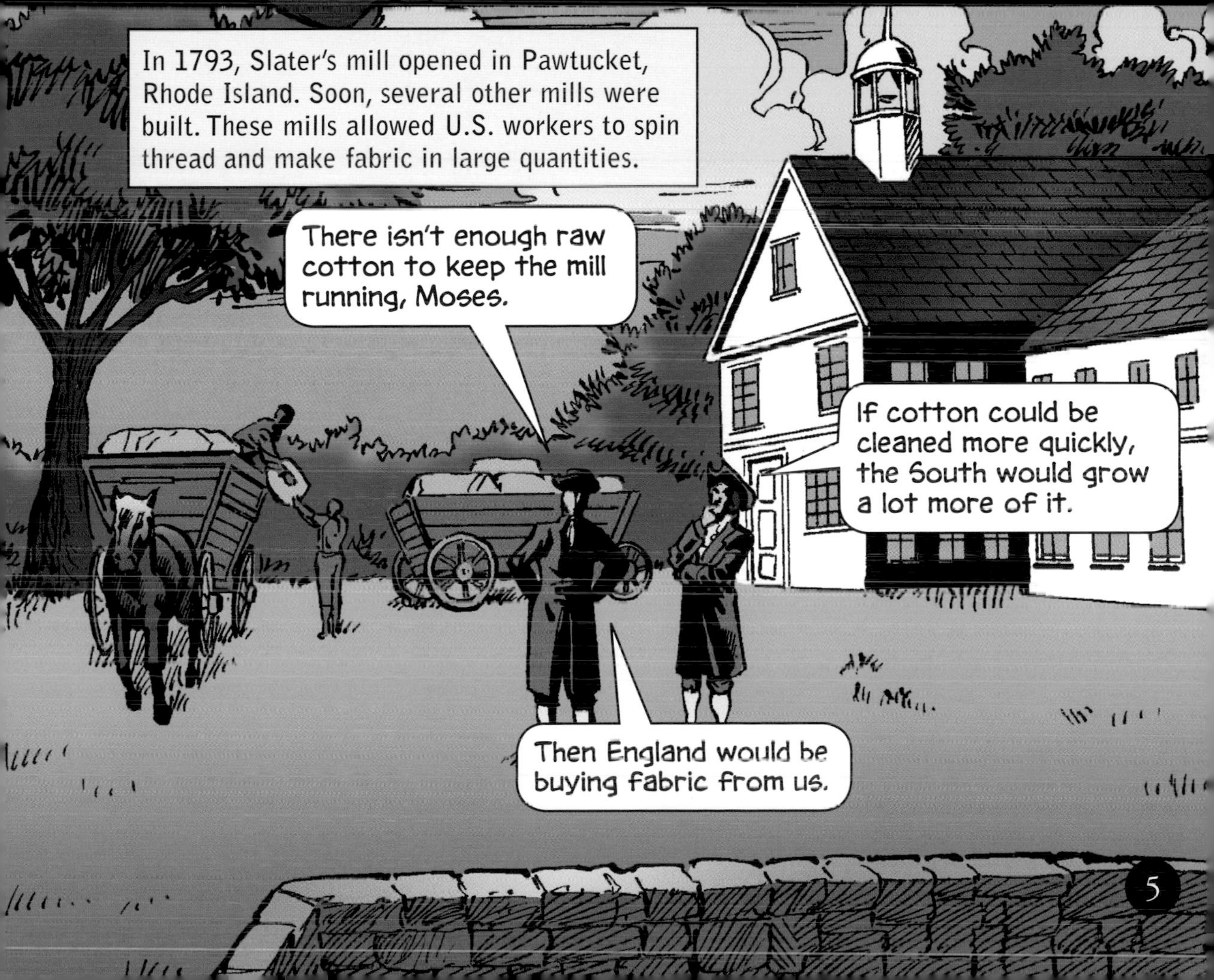
In 1793, Slater's mill opened in Pawtucket, Rhode Island. Soon, several other mills were built. These mills allowed U.S. workers to spin thread and make fabric in large quantities.
There isn't enough raw cotton to keep the mill running, Moses.
If cotton could be cleaned more quickly, the South would grow a lot more of it.
Then England would be buying fabric from us.

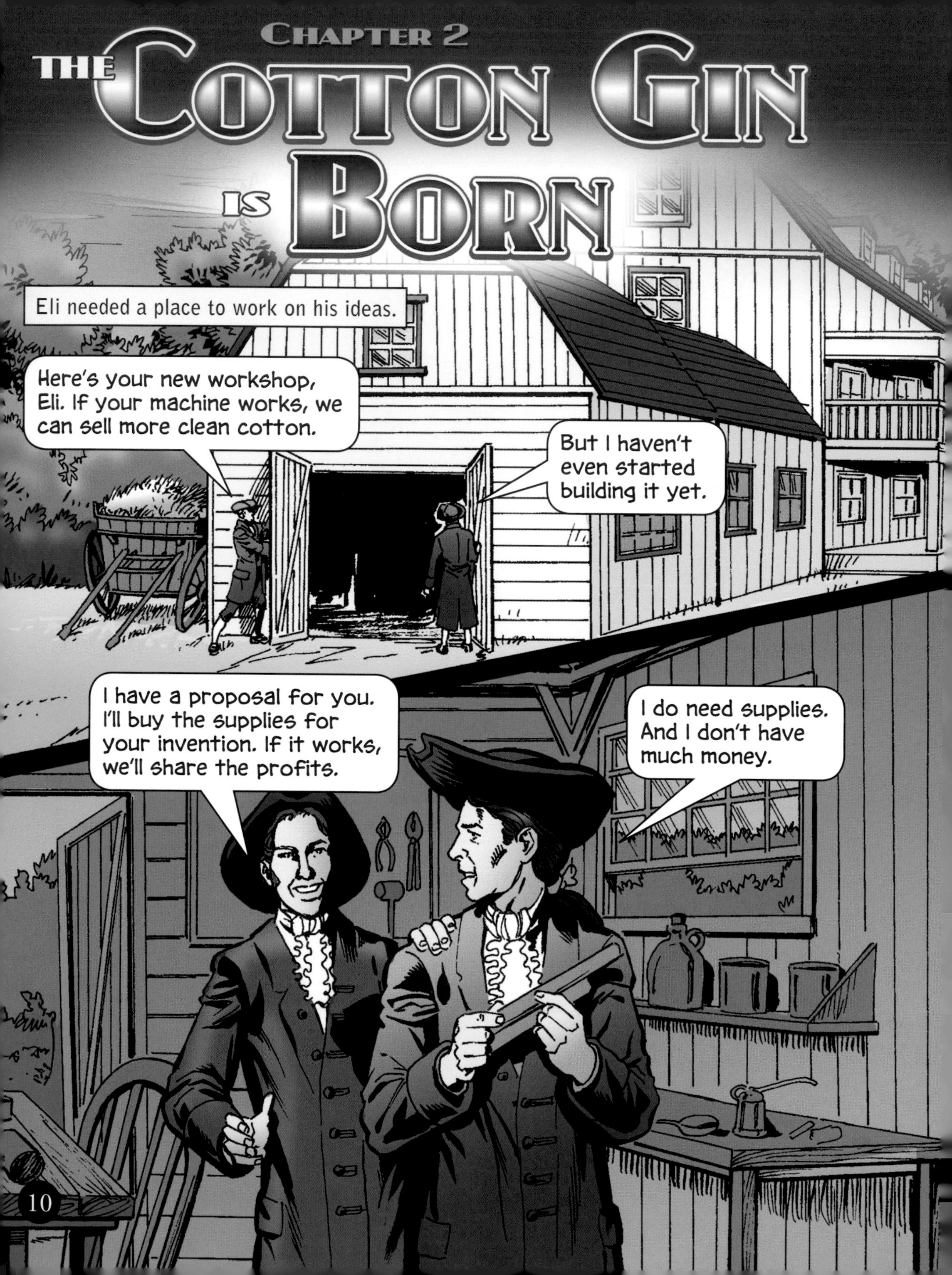

Chapter 2
The Cotton Gin is Born
Eli needed a place to work on his ideas.
Here's your new workshop, Eli. If your machine works, we can sell more clean cotton.
But I haven't even started building it yet.
I have a proposal for you. I'll buy the supplies for your invention. If it works, we'll share the profits.
I do need supplies. And I don't have much money.

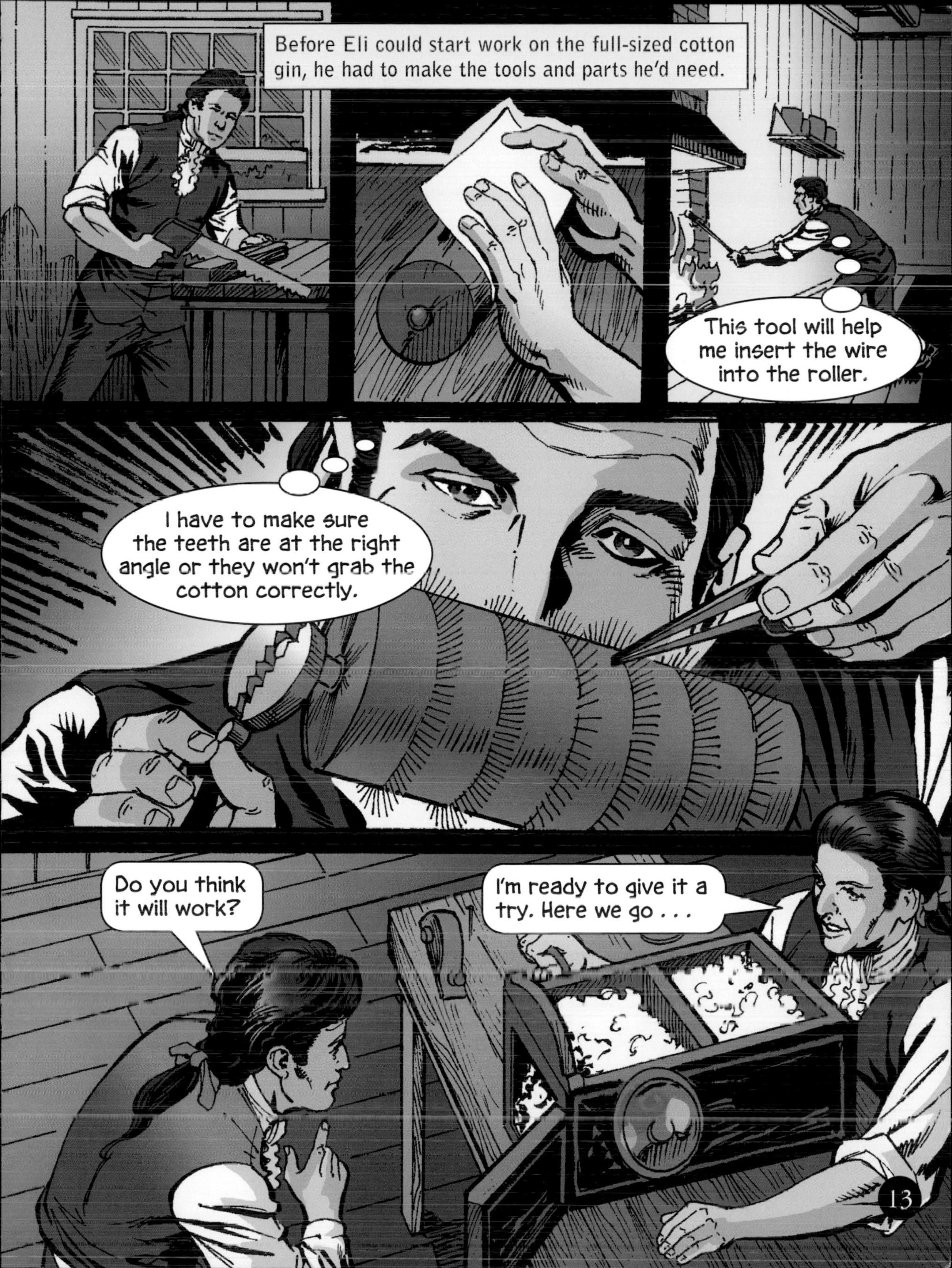
Before Eli could start work on the full-sized cotton gin, he had to make the tools and parts he'd need.
This tool will help me insert the wire into the roller.
I have to make sure the teeth are at the right angle or they won't grab the cotton correctly.
Do you think it will work?
I'm ready to give it a try. Here we go . . .

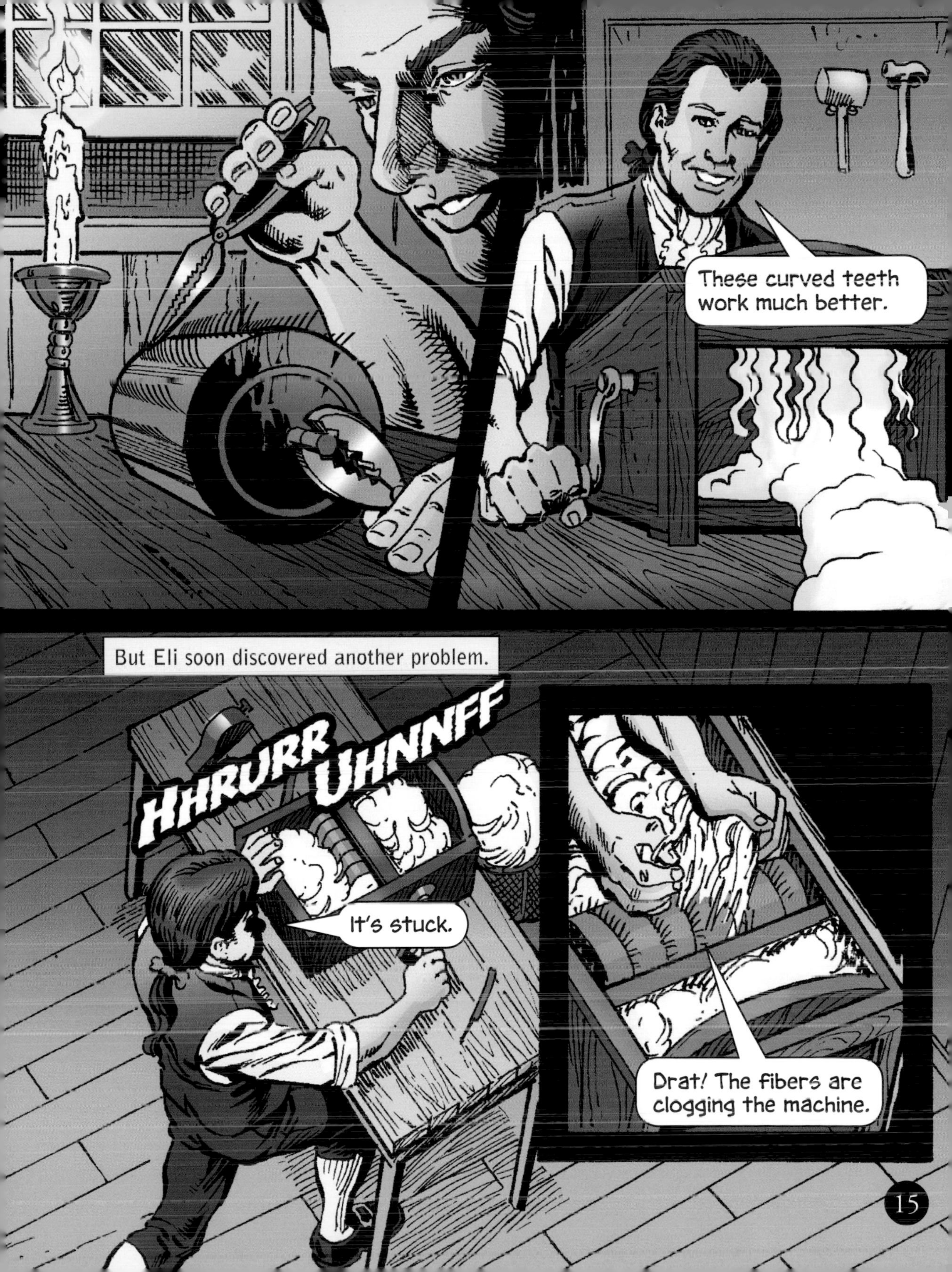
These curved teeth work much better.
But Eli soon discovered another problem.
HHRURR
UHNNFF
It's stuck.
Drat! The fibers are clogging the machine.

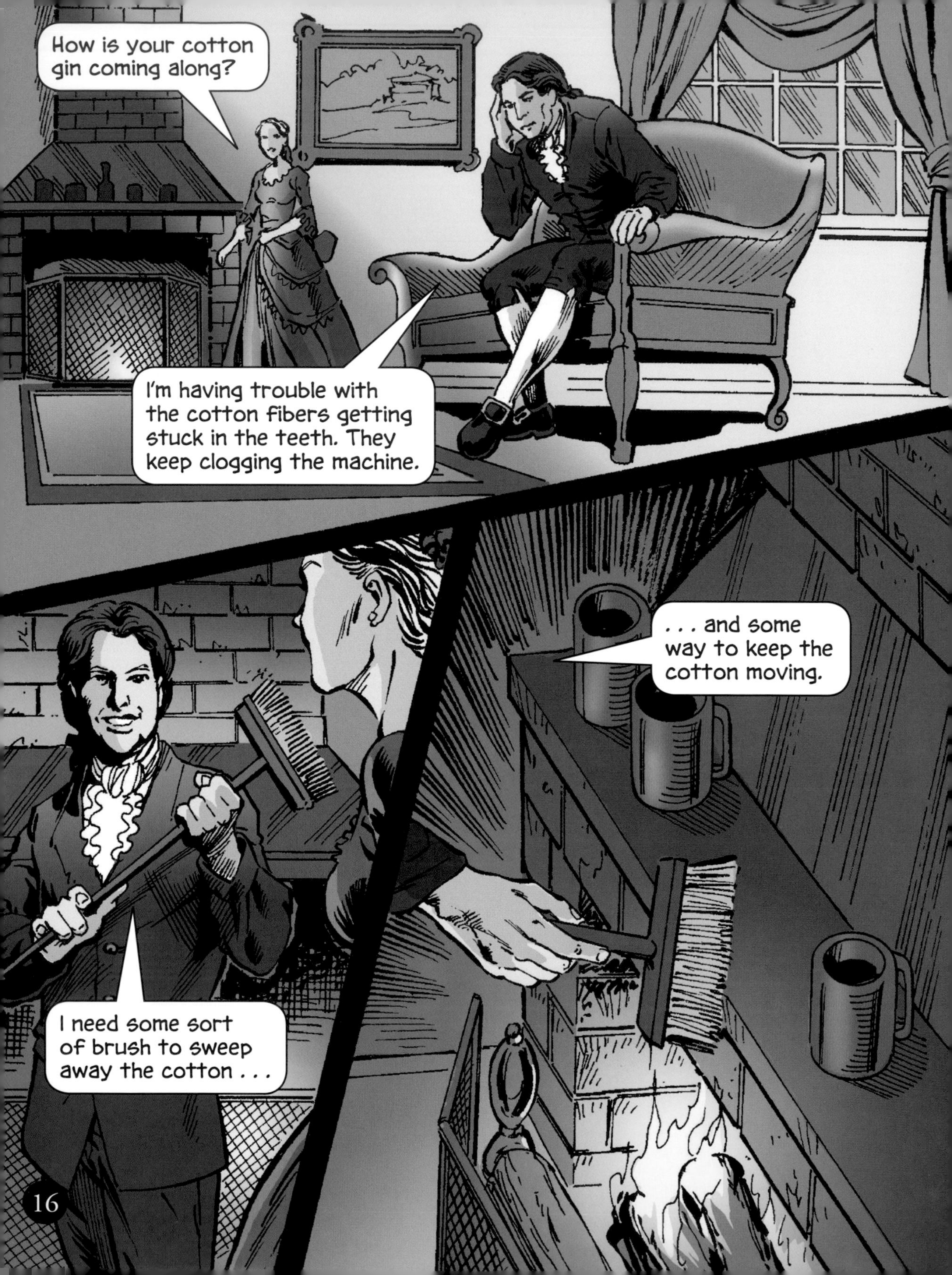
How is your cotton gin coming along?
I'm having trouble with the cotton fibers getting stuck in the teeth. They keep clogging the machine.
I need some sort of brush to sweep away the cotton . . .
. . . and some way to keep the cotton moving.

Chapter 3
A Stolen Idea

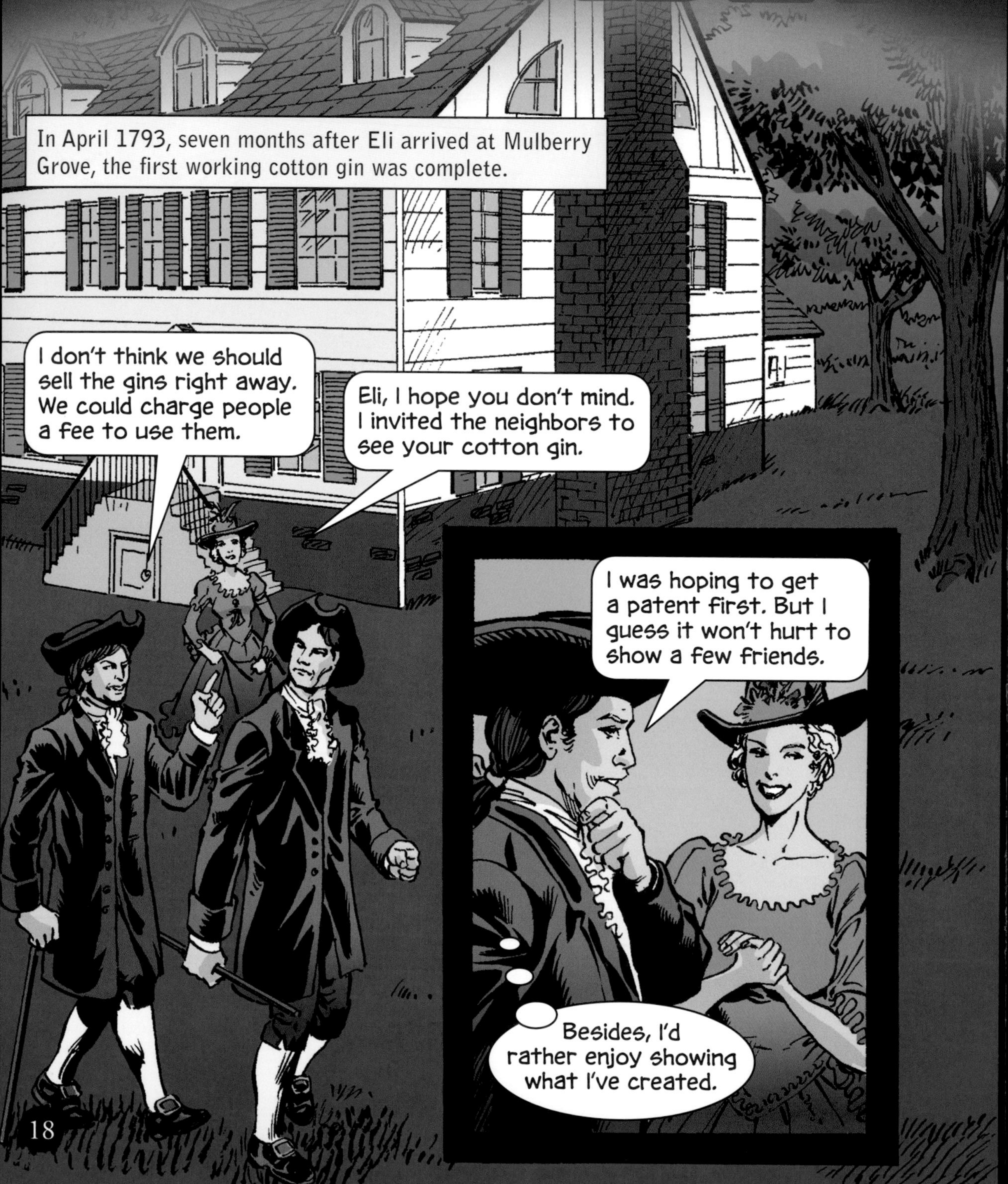

In April 1793, seven months after Eli arrived at Mulberry Grove, the first working cotton gin was complete.
I don't think we should sell the gins right away. We could charge people a fee to use them.
Eli, I hope you don't mind. I invited the neighbors to see your cotton gin.
I was hoping to get a patent first. But I guess it won't hurt to show a few friends.
Besides, I'd rather enjoy showing what I've created.

Chapter 4
The Cost of a Dream

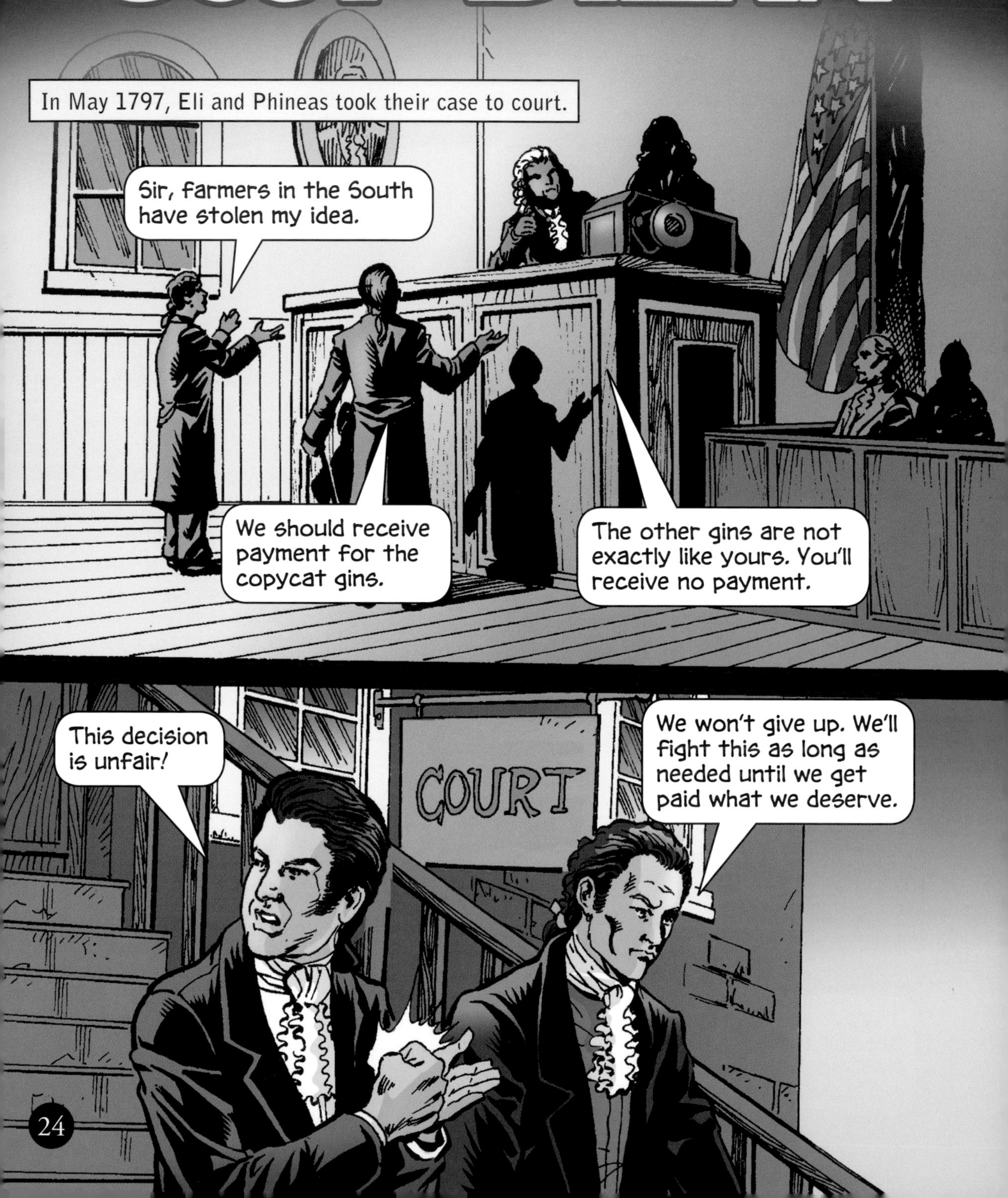
In May 1797, Eli and Phineas took their case to court.
Sir, farmers in the South have stolen my idea.
We should receive payment for the copycat gins.
The other gins are not exactly like yours. You'll receive no payment.
This decision is unfair!
COURT
We won't give up. We'll fight this as long as needed until we get paid what we deserve.

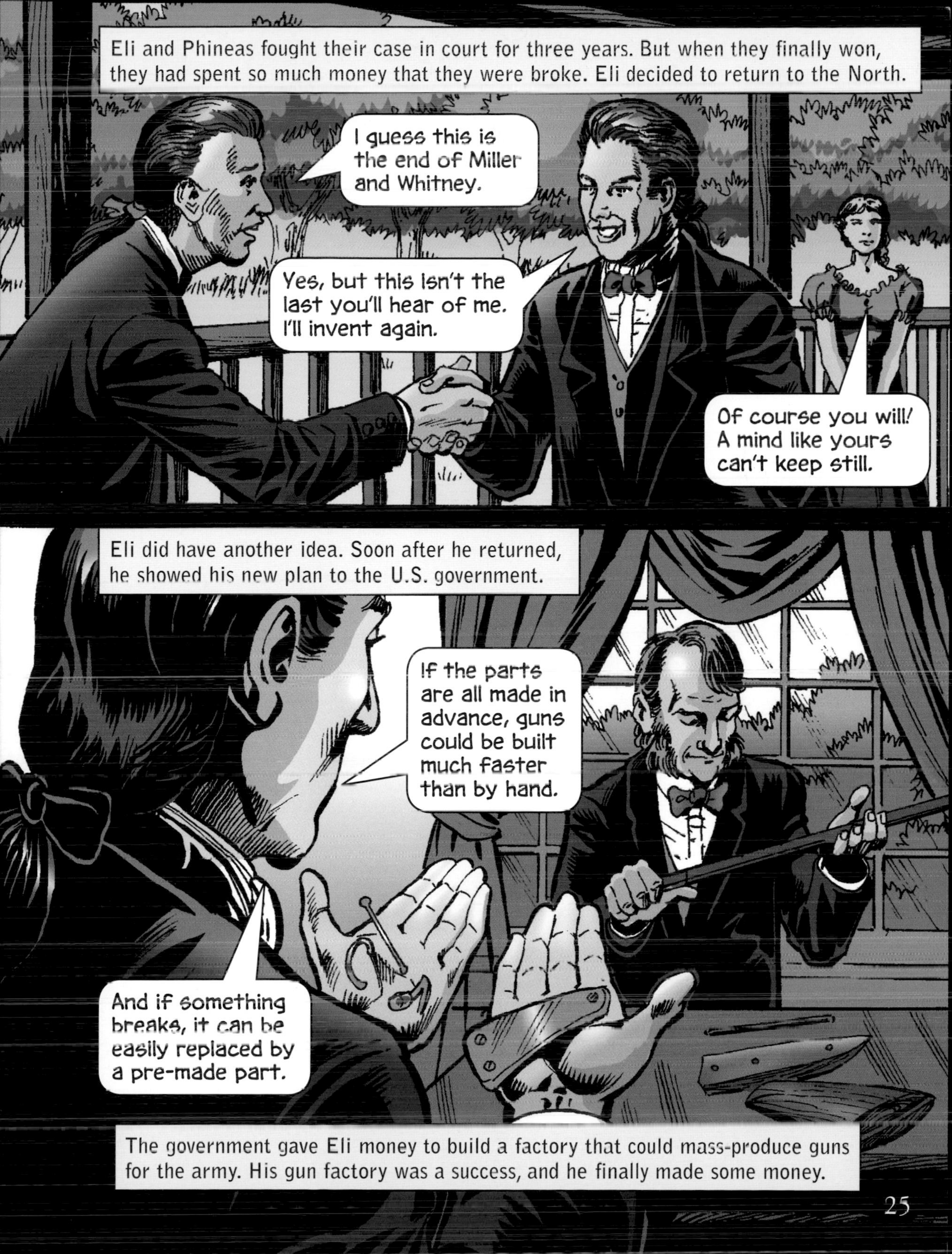
Eli and Phineas fought their case in court for three years. But when they finally won, they had spent so much money that they were broke. Eli decided to return to the North.
I guess this is the end of Miller and Whitney.
Yes, but this isn't the last you'll hear of me. I'll invent again.
Of course you will! A mind like yours can't keep still.
Eli did have another idea. Soon after he returned, he showed his new plan to the U.S. government.
If the parts are all made in advance, guns could be built much faster than by hand.
And if something breaks, it can be easily replaced by a pre-made part.
The government gave Eli money to build a factory that could mass-produce guns for the army. His gun factory was a success, and he finally made some money.

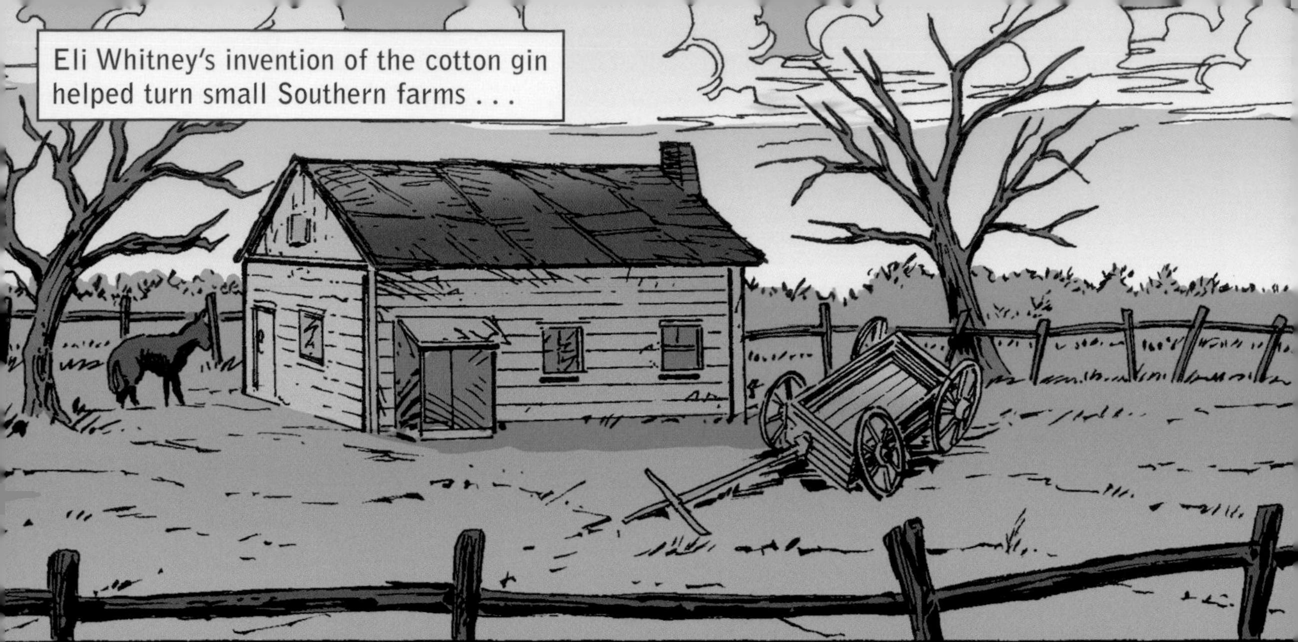
Eli Whitney's invention of the cotton gin helped turn small Southern farms . . .
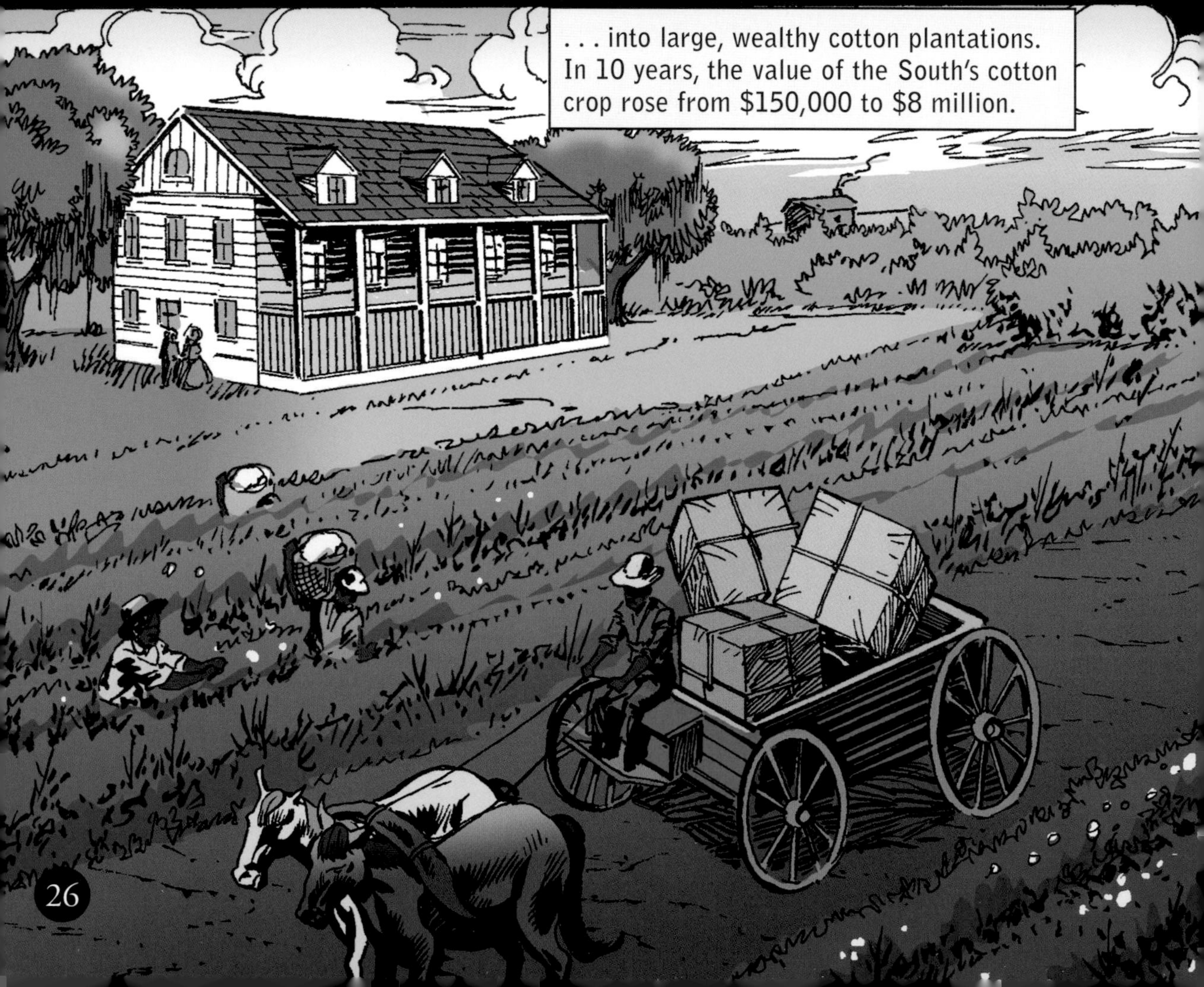
. . . into large, wealthy cotton plantations. In 10 years, the value of the South's cotton crop rose from $150,000 to $8 million.

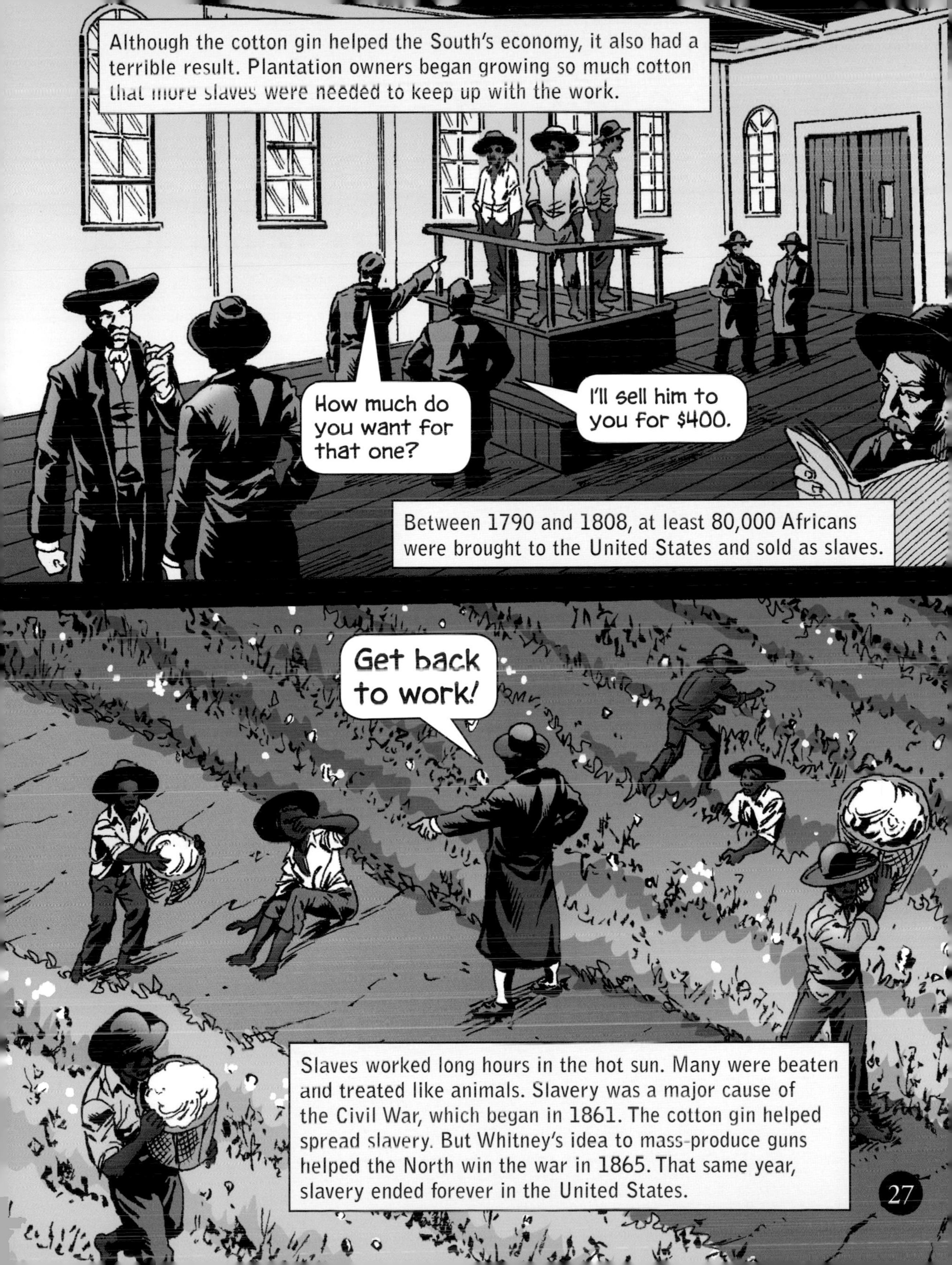
Although the cotton gin helped the South's economy, it also had a terrible result. Plantation owners began growing so much cotton that more slaves were needed to keep up with the work.
How much do you want for that one?
I'll sell him to you for $400.
Between 1790 and 1808, at least 80,000 Africans were brought to the United States and sold as slaves.
Get back to work!
Slaves worked long hours in the hot sun. Many were beaten and treated like animals. Slavery was a major cause of the Civil War, which began in 1861. The cotton gin helped spread slavery. But Whitney's idea to mass-produce guns helped the North win the war in 1865. That same year, slavery ended forever in the United States.

ELI WHITNEY AND THE COTTON GIN

 Eli Whitney was born December 8, 1765, in Westborough, Massachusetts. He died January 8, 1825, in New Haven, Connectictut.

 In cotton gin, the word "gin" is short for "engine."

 Hodgen Holmes made cotton gins similar to Eli Whitney's. Holmes used a saw instead of wire teeth in his cotton gin. Because he used a saw, the courts ruled that it was a different invention, not a stolen one.

 After their legal battles, Eli and Phineas decided to sell the cotton gins instead of charging farmers to use them. The farmers were satisfied with this idea and bought many of the cotton gins.

 Phineas Miller and Catherine Greene were married in 1796. They had so many financial troubles that they had to sell the plantation in 1800. Mulberry Grove sold for only $15,000.

The ability to easily clean green-seed cotton with the cotton gin caused slavery to spread in the South. In 1790 there were six slave states. By 1860 there were 15 slave states.

 The cotton gin is still used to clean cotton. Today's cotton gins are similar to Eli Whitney's but use electric motors, rather than men or horses, to power them.

 Clothing is not the only cotton product. Cotton is also used in blankets, tents, and even dollar bills. Cottonseed oil is used in cooking oil, salad dressing, crackers, and cookies.

 Eli Whitney's idea to use interchangeable parts to mass-produce products is still being used today. From small toys to large machines, almost everything is built using this method.

GLOSSARY

boll (BOHL)—a round pod on some plants that contains seeds

fiber (FYE-bur)—a long, thin thread of material, such as cotton, wool, or silk

patent (PAT-uhnt)—a legal document giving an inventor sole rights to make and sell an item he or she invented

plantation (plan-TAY-shuhn)—a large farm where one main crop is grown, such as coffee, tobacco, or cotton

profit (PROF-it)—the amount of money left after all the costs of running a business have been subtracted

reestablish (ree-ess-TAB-lish)—to set up again

INTERNET SITES

FactHound offers a safe, fun way to find Internet sites related to this book. All of the sites on FactHound have been researched by our staff.

Here's how:
1. Visit *www.facthound.com*
2. Choose your grade level.
3. Type in this book ID **0736868437** for age-appropriate sites. You may also browse subjects by clicking on letters, or by clicking on pictures and words.
4. Click on the **Fetch It** button.

FactHound will fetch the best sites for you!